Giant Trucks

KATIE MARSICO

Children's Press®
An Imprint of Scholastic Inc.

Content Consultant
Matthew Lammi, PhD
Assistant Professor
Department of Science, Technology,
Engineering, and Mathematics Education
North Carolina State University
Raleigh, North Carolina

Library of Congress Cataloging-in-Publication Data
Marsico, Katie, 1980– author.
 Giant trucks / by Katie Marsico.
   pages cm. — (A true book)
 Summary: "Learn all about the world's biggest, toughest trucks, from how they were invented to
what jobs they are used to perform today."— Provided by publisher.
 ISBN 978-0-531-22481-6 (library binding : alk. paper) — ISBN 978-0-531-22271-3 (pbk. : alk. paper)
 1. Trucks—Juvenile literature. I. Title. II. Series: True book.
 TL230.15.M3665 2016
 629.225—dc23   2015029116

© 2016 Scholastic Inc.
All rights reserved. Published in 2016 by Children's Press, an imprint of Scholastic Inc.
Printed in China 62
SCHOLASTIC, CHILDREN'S PRESS, A TRUE BOOK™, and associated logos are trademarks and/or
registered trademarks of Scholastic Inc.
1 2 3 4 5 6 7 8 9 10 R 25 24 23 22 21 20 19 18 17 16

**Front cover: A dump truck is loading with
rocks in a quarry
Back cover: An off-road recovery vehicle**

Find the Truth!

Everything you are about to read is true *except* for one of the sentences on this page.

Which one is **TRUE**?

T or F The earliest trucks were powered by diesel engines.

T or F Drivers need special licenses to operate giant trucks.

Find the answers in this book.

Contents

From Spilled Syrup to Confused Cows

Some giant trucks have tires that are much larger than the average person.

This crane can lift 1,200 tons — the same as 12 blue whales!

Construction jobs require a wide range of giant trucks.

CHAPTER 1

Massive Movers

Workers are building a community center in a local park, and the construction site is whirring with activity. Cement mixers blend sand, gravel, and water to make concrete. Dump trucks haul away debris. Meanwhile, a towering mobile crane raises and lowers construction materials. Thanks to these giant trucks, residents will be able to enjoy their new community center soon!

Some giant trucks are built on-site in construction zones.

Some giant trucks must cross rough terrain in order to reach their destinations.

Heavy-Duty Hauling

Cement mixers, dump trucks, and mobile cranes are examples of large vehicles that are often called giant or heavy-duty trucks. The term also applies to a wide variety of other vehicles that rumble both on and off roadways every day. These engineering wonders include garbage trucks, tank trucks, heavy haulers, and ballast tractors.

A heavy-duty truck is defined by its gross vehicle weight (GVW). The GVW is the maximum weight a truck is able to carry. It includes the weight of a vehicle itself, as well as its fuel, driver, passengers, and the payload, or **cargo**, it transports. Most giant trucks have a GVW greater than 26,000 pounds (11,793 kilograms). Some have a GVW of more than 33,000 pounds (14,969 kg)!

Some of the world's heaviest trucks are the dump trucks used at mining sites.

Making Transportation More Efficient

Whatever their GVW, all giant trucks serve an important purpose. They make it easier for people to lift and carry heavy loads. Without these vehicles, it would be far more difficult to transport cargo and do construction work. With their help, trade, transportation, and industries ranging from waste management to land development take much less time and effort.

Some truck trailers can be loaded from the side.

An employee checks the engine of a giant truck at a factory in India.

Giant trucks have evolved a great deal over time and will continue to do so in the future. Engineers work to design vehicles that are both powerful and environmentally friendly. Their efforts build on an exciting history filled with **innovations**, or changes. Such changes and improvements have helped shape these massive engineering wonders.

Horse-drawn carts transported most goods in the 19th century, particularly in towns and cities.

A History of Giant Trucks

Before the late 19th century, horse-drawn carts and wagons transported most of the goods traveling over land. However, such vehicles could carry only a limited amount of weight. They also didn't operate at high speeds. Trains moved some cargo, but trains couldn't reach areas that lacked railroad tracks.

 Horses hauled everything from heavy freight to ice and milk.

Alternatives to Horses and Trains

In the late 1800s, inventors developed steam-powered trucks. These vehicles didn't depend on horses or railroad tracks to function. Known as steam wagons, they gained popularity in Europe and the United States. Then in the 1890s, engineers started designing trucks with internal combustion engines. An internal combustion engine produces power by burning a fuel such as gasoline or oil. These engines provided more energy with less fuel than steam wagons and soon became more common.

Steam-powered vehicles were put to a number of different uses, including the transport and delivery of goods.

A man drives a delivery truck loaded with meat through Washington, D.C., in the 1920s.

Fuel-powered trucks were faster and stronger than horse-drawn vehicles. Not all roadways, however, were designed to accommodate them. The many dirt and cobblestone roads of the time were better suited to horse hooves than truck tires. Fortunately, this changed after the turn of the 20th century as more towns and cities began building paved streets. As they did so, the number of truck manufacturers grew in both Europe and the United States.

Wartime Trucks

World War I (1914–1918) helped speed along the evolution of larger trucks. Military units started using such vehicles to transport **ammunition** and other supplies. These trucks needed to be as sturdy, powerful, and efficient as possible. With this in mind, engineers rapidly improved engine and truck design. About two decades later, World War II (1939–1945) provided another, similar boost to giant truck technology.

A Timeline of Truck Development

1769

The first fully self-powered vehicle is built to haul military weapons. Its engine relies on steam power.

1893

Rudolf Diesel builds the first working experimental model of a diesel engine.

Additional Innovations

During the 1950s, diesel engines became a standard feature on trucks. An engine can convert more energy from diesel than from other fuels, such as gasoline. For this reason, diesel engines are frequently considered a better choice for larger vehicles. Diesel engines allow trucks to travel faster, farther, and with even greater loads than gasoline engines do.

1896
The first motorized truck, produced by Gottlieb Daimler (above), takes to the roads.

1898
Alexander Winton develops the first semi, or tractor-trailer truck.

1912
The Lincoln Highway, the first U.S. highway to reach from coast to coast, opens.

Truck designs have improved over the years to make vehicles faster, stronger, and more efficient.

Today, giant trucks are more efficient than ever. **Aerodynamic** designs reduce wind resistance, so trucks use less fuel as they travel. Highway systems and **container shipping** allow trucks to haul more cargo farther and faster than before. Trucks' numerous shapes and sizes suit a variety of purposes. A huge arm can lift construction materials or a giant tank can transport flammable liquids. Massive cargo holds can do anything from shift earth to haul live animals.

Heavy-Duty Driving

As giant trucks have evolved, so have the rules about their use. After all, controlling more than 26,000 pounds (11,793 kg) of vehicle is no easy task. For example, rounding a corner in an 18-wheel tractor-trailer is different from turning a smaller four-wheel car. People who are interested in driving giant trucks therefore usually undergo training. Then they obtain a special type of license called a **commercial** driver's license (CDL).

20

CDL TRAINING

The cab is full of knobs, wheels, switches, and buttons that control the truck's various systems.

CHAPTER 3

Rumbling Along

Giant trucks share certain features with one another. These include a chassis, which is a vehicle's basic framework, and a cab where the driver sits. Giant trucks have **axles**, wheels, and an engine. They also have an area where cargo is stored. Sometimes, this is in a trailer. Giant trucks operate using a combination of electricity, air pressure, and water pressure. These systems control a truck's steering, brakes, lights, lifting or moving attachments, and other functions.

 Some truck drivers are on the road up to 14 hours a day.

Space-Saving Compactors

Some giant trucks have unique features. For example, garbage trucks typically include some kind of compactor. A compactor squeezes and flattens waste into smaller bundles. This squeezing helps conserve, or save, space. Why is this important? In the United States alone, residents create enough trash to fill 63,000 garbage trucks every day. Garbage trucks transport all this waste!

A compactor pushes down on the waste in a garbage truck.

A worker positions a cement truck mixer's chute so concrete pours in the proper place.

Mobile Mixers

Like garbage trucks, cement mixers include their own innovative features. One is a giant steel or fiberglass drum. Inside this drum, a rotating, or turning, blade blends the ingredients for concrete, a mixture of cement and rock. Once a cement mixer arrives at a building site, the thick, sticky mixture inside the drum is forced out. It travels through chutes or special pumps to a sidewalk, a building foundation, or other location. There, it is left to set, or harden.

Cranes are common on construction sites.

Tall and Easy to Transport

The most unique feature on a mobile crane is the crane itself. A crane is a tall machine that is used to lift and move heavy objects. It works by suspending, or hanging, a load from a long-reaching arm. One of the advantages of a mobile crane is that the crane is attached to a truck. It is therefore easy to transport to and from building sites.

Built to Hold a Lot of Liquid

As a tank truck's name implies, its best-known feature is a tank. This container is made of stainless steel and usually has a cylindrical (tube-like) or square shape. Most tank trucks are designed to hold up to 12,000 gallons (45,425 liters) of liquid. Tank trucks may transport anything from fuel and liquid waste to water, milk, and juice.

A worker opens a fire hydrant to fill his tank truck with water.

Hauling Houses

Tractor units are trucks specially designed to pull a trailer or other separate cargo attached to its back. All giant trucks have engines, but a tractor unit has a particularly powerful towing engine. This feature allows it to haul especially heavy loads. Tractor units can often function off paved roads. They might be used for military or commercial purposes. For example, heavy haulers are able to transport huge telescope parts and even entire houses!

A house must be well secured to the trailer when transported by truck.

Ballast tractors are a type of tractor unit. The wheels of these giant trucks have excellent traction, or grip, on the road. This is because a heavy material known as ballast is added over the wheels. The weight of the ballast prevents the wheels from slipping. This added traction helps the truck move heavy loads such as large sections of bridges and ships.

From Spilled Syrup to Confused Cows

Giant trucks carry all kinds of cargo. When these massive vehicles are involved in accidents, major messes often result. These stories illustrate the many items that giant trucks transport. They also demonstrate what happens when a drive doesn't go precisely as planned.

Boxes of Bees

In April 2015, a truck in Washington overturned on the highway. Fortunately, no one was injured. Unfortunately, the truck was carrying roughly 14 million live honeybees! Local beekeepers attempted to retrieve the insects. However thousands of insects escaped to the wild.

A Sticky Situation

In June 2015, an overturned tank truck spilled 1,600 gallons (6,057 L) of maple syrup onto a road in New Jersey. The sticky spill, which mixed with diesel fuel that had leaked from the truck, spread across 50 square yards (42 square meters). No one was injured, but cleanup was complicated. Removing syrup from a roadway generally involves using sand to soak it up.

Happy Holidays!

In December 2014, an 18-wheel Federal Express (FedEx) delivery truck overturned in Georgia. There were no serious injuries. However, hundreds of packages—many containing holiday presents—lay scattered all over the road. Within about six hours, workers had cleared the items. FedEx employees later inspected the shipments to assess any damage.

Cattle Chaos

In April 2015, a tractor unit transporting cattle overturned in Illinois. Rescuers worked to free animals trapped in the trailers following the accident. Workers also struggled to corral 12 cows that had escaped. The incident temporarily snarled traffic wherever the confused cattle wandered.

CHAPTER 4

The Wildest Wheeled Giants

All giant trucks are impressive, but some are absolutely extreme! A prime example is the BelAZ 75710. This massive dump truck operates in a coal mine in the rugged Russian province of Siberia. It is able to move roughly 450 tons of dirt and other materials at once. That's about the same weight as seven fully fueled and loaded narrow-bodied jet airliners!

The BelAZ 75710 was first revealed in 2013.

31

Super-Sized Truck

The BelAZ 75710 is frequently described as the world's largest dump truck. It is powered by five diesel engines, which provide energy to four electric motors. At its top speed, when its bed is empty, the vehicle can move at about 40 miles (64 kilometers) per hour. It's as long as two double-decker buses and features eight gigantic wheels. Each of the BelAZ 75710's enormous tires is more than twice as tall as the average person!

Bed or box holding cargo

The BelAZ 75710 requires a great deal of power to lift its bed and empty out any materials the truck is hauling.

Cab where driver sits

8 wheels, 4 on each side

Though it hauled cargo in the 1990s, the Red Giant's trailer is usually empty today.

The Remarkable Red Giant

The owners of a giant truck in Wisconsin claim they operate the world's longest semitrailer truck. A semitrailer truck, or semi, consists of a tractor and a half-trailer that has wheels only on its back end. Named the Red Giant, the semi in Wisconsin measures 93 feet (28 meters) long. Its **wheelbase** alone is 36 feet (11 m).

The Red Giant can play sounds to go with the ads shown on its screens.

As a result of the Red Giant's sheer size, its owners came up with a rather remarkable idea. They outfitted each side of the truck with an 11-foot (3.4 m) **light-emitting diode** (LED) monitor. These screens serve as moving billboards. For a fee, businesses can place advertisements along the sides of the Red Giant. Such ads are then seen everywhere the truck travels.

Long and Strong

What's strong enough to lift the weight of 700 cars? The LTM 11200-9.1 mobile crane is equipped to raise and lower this much weight. This mobile crane is considered the most powerful in the world. The truck moves at a maximum speed of 47 miles per hour (76 kph). Its heaviest load can be about 1,200 tons.

Even when the crane's arm is collapsed to its shortest length, the LTM 11200-9.1 is huge.

The LTM 11200-9.1 has the world's longest telescopic boom. A telescopic boom is a pole or rod that can extend or collapse by having sections that slide inside one another. When stretched to its full length, the boom on the LTM 11200-9.1 measures 328 feet (100 m) long. So far, this mobile crane has mainly been used to install equipment on wind farms. Wind farms use the wind to generate, or create, electricity.

The LTM 11200-9.1's arm can be extended, collapsed, and locked in place automatically.

Monsters Versus Giants

Many people are probably familiar with the term *monster truck*. It describes an oversized pickup truck that has extremely large tires. Monster trucks are often driven in exhibitions where they demolish smaller vehicles for entertainment. Yet they're not nearly as large as giant trucks. Monster trucks generally weigh between 9,000 and 12,500 pounds (4,082 and 5,670 kg). That's just a fraction of what the smallest heavy-duty commercial truck weighs!

A range of companies—
located around the
world design and
build giant trucks.

CHAPTER 5

Down the Road

For decades, giant trucks have demonstrated their importance in making transportation efficient. Today, engineers continue to work on designs that will support this legacy far into the future. Engineers must address other considerations as well. One of their biggest concerns today is creating giant trucks that are environmentally friendly.

Some giant trucks cost millions of dollars to buy new.

Vehicle engines produce exhaust, which contains a variety of harmful gases.

The Problem of Pollution

Many modern automobiles run on diesel fuel or gasoline. Unfortunately, when such fuel is burned, the engines release certain gases that harm the environment. Giant trucks require more fuel to run than do smaller vehicles. Conservationists are especially worried about the amount of pollutants these trucks produce. As a result, engineers are developing methods of making giant trucks that use less or different fuel.

In some cases, manufacturers have already taken important steps to achieve this goal. For example, most giant trucks are currently equipped with low-rolling-resistance tires. Such tires reduce **friction**. Less friction means the vehicle uses less energy to stay in motion. As a result, low-rolling-resistance tires cut back on the amount of fuel a giant truck needs to operate.

Low-rolling-resistance tires help make a giant truck more efficient.

Employees assemble diesel engines at KAMAZ, one of the largest giant truck producers in Russia.

Engineers have also experimented with altering the temperature at which diesel engines burn fuel. By lowering this temperature, it's possible to reduce the amount of harmful gases the engine produces.

These advancements are just the beginning. Engineers continue to work toward additional discoveries and developments that will help create even more environmentally friendly giant trucks.

Forever Moving Forward

Centuries ago, it was probably hard to imagine massive fuel-powered trucks replacing horse-drawn carts. Nevertheless, these engineering wonders have forever reshaped the way materials are moved. From towering mobile cranes to winding tractor units, giant trucks will continue to help people move forward for generations to come. ★

A person poses for a photo in the wheel of a BelAZ truck during a visit to the factory.

Minimum gross vehicle weight (GVW) of most giant trucks: 26,000 lbs (11,793 kg)

Maximum liquid capacity of most tank trucks: 12,000 gal (45,425 L)

Amount of dirt the BelAZ 75710 can move at once: Roughly 450 tons

Number of engines and motors that power the BelAZ 75710: 8

Length of the Red Giant: 93 ft. (28 m)

Wheelbase of the Red Giant: 36 ft. (11 m)

Maximum weight the LTM 11200-9.1 is capable of raising and lowering: Approximately 1,200 tons

Full length of the telescopic boom on the LTM 11200-9.1: 328 ft. (100 m)

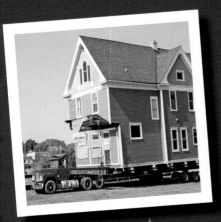

Did you find the truth?

F The earliest trucks were powered by diesel engines.

T Drivers need special licenses to operate giant trucks.

Resources

Books

Colson, Rob. *Trucks*. New York: PowerKids Press, 2013.

Gifford, Clive. *Super Trucks*. New York: DK Publishing, 2013.

Osier, Dan. *Dump Trucks*. New York: PowerKids Press, 2014.

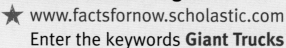

Visit this Scholastic Web site for more information on giant trucks:
★ www.factsfornow.scholastic.com
Enter the keywords **Giant Trucks**

Important Words

aerodynamic (air-oh-dye-NAM-ik) — designed to move through the air very easily and quickly

ammunition (am-yuh-NISH-uhn) — things such as bullets or shells that can be fired from weapons

axles (AK-suhlz) — rods in the center of wheels, around which a wheel turns

cargo (KAHR-goh) — freight that is carried by a truck, train, ship, or aircraft

commercial (kuh-MUR-shuhl) — of or having to do with making money

container shipping (kuhn-TAY-ner SHIP-ing) — transporting items in large, standard-sized containers via truck, train, ship, or aircraft

friction (FRIK-shuhn) — the force that slows down objects when they rub against each other

innovations (in-uh-VAY-shuhnz) — new ideas or inventions

light-emitting diode (LITE i-MIT-ing DYE-ohd) — a small light, usually of a single color, that turns on when electricity passes through it

overturned (oh-vur-TURND) — turned upside down or on its side

wheelbase (WEEL-bayss) — the distance between a vehicle's front and rear wheels

Index

Page numbers in **bold** indicate illustrations.

About the Author

Katie Marsico graduated from Northwestern University and worked as an editor in reference publishing before she began writing in 2006. Since that time, she has published more than 200 titles for children and young adults. Ms. Marsico is extremely grateful for the giant trucks that pick up her family's trash and recycling every Wednesday.